POLO:

, RULES OF THE GAME

IONS ON HOW TO PLAY

BY WILLIAM HENRY

THE game of water-polo has perhaps done more during recent years to popularise and to cause an interest to be taken in swimming than any other branch of the sport. It is essentially a game for swimmers, and one that affords no lack of opportunity for the exhibition of skill and the development of staying power. Its practice tends to improve the speed rates of all those who participate in the pastime, as well as to inculcate in the minds of its followers good ideas as to the best methods of obtaining command over the water. In long-distance swims only one style of swimming is, as a rule, adopted, but in water-polo the rapid changes of position which are necessary compel players to constantly alter their style. This is in itself a beneficial phase of the game, and one which teaches a swimmer how complete may become his power.

It was not for this reason, as may be easily imagined, that the game was first promoted, but merely for the purpose of providing something new and attractive at swimming galas ; and with this view, on May 12, 1870, a committee was appointed by the Swimming Association, then known as the London Swimming Association, to draw up a code of rules for the management of the game of 'football in the water.' As recently as 1887, in an American work on 'Swimming and Life-saving,' water-polo was described under the heading of 'Ornamental Swimming.' Prior to 1877, various attempts were made by individual swimmers to arrange some kind of ball game in the water, and at many entertainments and swimming matches what was termed water base-ball was played, the sides usually consisting of not more than three players.

There were a few matches played in 1876, but it is difficult to obtain definite particulars, as but few of them were reported. The Rowing Club at Bournemouth played in that year, and it is interesting to note the method in which these almost pre-historic games were played at a time when most of the present exponents were in the nursery or at school. A newspaper of that period informs us that the Bournemouth Premier Rowing Club carried out the 'first of a series of aquatic hand-ball matches' on Thursday, July 13, 1876, off the pier. Curiously enough, there were seven competitors on each side, and the 'goals were marked by four flags, moored at the west of the pier, 50 yards apart.' After a 'severe struggle,' the ball burst; but the players, nothing daunted, and 'properly habited, displayed their aquatic accomplishments for some time.' A week later, so another newspaper-cutting informs us, 'twelve members of the club proceeded in rowing galleys, and took up a position near their goals, which were marked out by flags describing an oblong of 60 yards by 40 yards. All being ready, an india-rubber ball, evidently the inside of an ordinary football, was placed in the centre between the parties, and a signal given, upon which both crews sprang with commendable agility from their galleys and struck out for the ball of conten-tion.' The report goes on to describe the battle, during which an incident occurred recalling the method adopted under their old rules by the Scotch goal-keepers. One player 'got a lucky hit which sent the ball back from his goal several yards, and it seemed as if his crew were, for a time, to have their own way;' but a player on the other side, 'who, instead of jumping in with his party, in the first instance, remained in his goal as backstock, now plunged in and reinforced his crew, who, after a short but obdurate tussle, turned the tide again in their favour. Again the ball burst, and, another not being forth-coming, the game was suspended.' Among those who were prominent in play were O. C. Mootham, W. J. and E. Worth, F. T. Cutler, H. Nash, H. Harvey, and J. A. Nethercoate, now highly respected and law-abiding burgesses of the new borough of Bournemouth. In these games it is amusing to note the length of the play, the size of the goals, the thin rubber ball that naturally could not last through the severe castigation it received, and the term 'backstock,' evidently coined from the writer's own imagination.

In the year 1877, before the annual competitions of the Bon Accord Club, which were to be held on the River Dee, the president of the club asked William Wilson, of Glasgow, whether the monotony of racing could not be varied by the institution of a game or competition which would amuse the spectator? The suggestion was acted upon : Mr. Wilson drew up a set of rules for a water game, termed 'aquatic football,' and play took place from bank to bank at the Bon Accord Festival. In the previous year Mr. Wilson drew up some rules for the Aberdeen Club. Later in the same year, the Victoria Baths and the West of Scotland Clubs played a game at the opening of the Victoria Baths. In October of the same year the rules were revised, and a competition extending over two nights was decided at Paisley Baths between the West of Scotland and Paisley Clubs. Paisley were beaten in the first match by one goal to *nil*, but in the return they vanquished their opponents, the score again being one goal to *nil*. The next year the rules were again revised for the Carnegie Club, and after this the West of Scotland paid some attention to the game. There were no goal-posts at first, the ball having to be played between two little flags placed eight or ten feet apart, and the game was merely a rough and tumble scramble from end to end of the field of play. Only soft india-rubber balls were used, and as they were often torn to pieces but little skill could be exercised. Keen followers of the sport soon began to recognise that this new game, if properly de-veloped would prove of immense service to the clubs in general, and they consulted together as to possible improvements. This led to the adoption of goal-posts similar to those used at football, and under these new conditions, in October 1879, at the first costume swimming entertainment ever held in Glasgow, the feature of the meeting was a match between the West of Scotland and Clyde Clubs, the teams consisting, as at present, of seven players each side. Ducking was not prohibited, but standing on the bottom of the bath or throwing with both hands was not allowed.

By this time the English clubs had begun to play a crude style of game, the Birmingham Leander, which was founded in 1877, and the Burton-on-Trent Amateur Club, started the following year, being among the first to adopt the new ball game as a club pastime.

There were no printed rules. The game was played with a small india-rubber hand-ball, about four or five inches in diameter. The goals were the ends of the bath, and the goal-keeper stood on the side; sometimes the captain ordered two goal-keepers, according to the width of the bath. The teams stood at the ends, and the ball was thrown into the centre. In those days the water was not over-clean, and the favourite trick was to place the ball inside the drawers, and swim to the other end, under water. The mode of scoring was to place the ball on the end of the bath with both hands, the forwards sometimes nearly having their neck broken by the goal-keeper jumping on the top of them, and at other times, when trying to score, the goal-keeper would lay hold of their hands and the ball, and drag them out of the water.

Match teams in 1879 consisted of about nine a side. The Dudley S. C. began playing Hanley about that year, and a season or two later the positions were taken after the Association Football system. In 1879 the width of the goals was limited to fourteen feet.

In June 1883, the secretary of the Birmingham Leander journeyed to Portsmouth at the invitation of Mr. Harry Fisk, the secretary of the local club, to confer as to the best methods of creating interest in water-polo, with the result that the following rules were agreed upon, and a match between Birmingham Leander and All-England arranged. The match was played on August 6, 1883, England winning by a goal to *nil*.

In the following year, England, captained by G. R. Bettinson (Regent), again beat Birmingham Leander by two goals to *nil*, and in 1885 defeated the Midland Counties Amateur Swimming Association by two touch downs to *nil*. The following rules were observed :

1. Duration of game, twenty minutes.
2. Captains to agree or toss for choice of goals.
3. At commencement of play, referee to throw ball into centre of course. All players shall then enter water immediately, except goal-keeper on either side. Goal-keeper may remain out and defend his goal as he may think best.
4. Ball may be passed from one player to another, and carried either on or below surface to goal.
5. No player to interfere with goal-keeper, either in or out of the water, or hold his opponents in any way, unless such goal-keeper, or opponents, are in possession of ball. In case of any player infringing this rule, a free throw to be at once given to his opponents from place where foul occurred.
6. A goal to be obtained by ball being taken up by hand and fairly placed on floating stage, or in boat provided for that purpose.
7. If during play ball goes out of course at side, referee shall immediately throw in same straight from where it goes out ; but if it goes out over or upon floating stage or boat, it shall immediately be taken up and thrown into play by goal-keeper upon stage or boat.
8. Umpires, or one of them, shall blow whistle immediately after a goal has been obtained, and play shall cease from that moment.
9. Teams to change goals at half-time.
10. Should any competitor who has been selected to take part in polo match fail to engage in same, he shall forfeit all prizes that at time of holding such match he may have already won at this festival, as well as any he may afterwards become entitled to in connection with same.
11. Power given to umpires, or, in case of dispute, to referee, to decide all circumstances not provided for by these rules.

A glance at these rules will show that they were most primitive in conception, especially Rule No. 10, and very simple as compared with those at present in vogue. A goal was obtainable by placing the ball on the end of the bath, or on a floating stage in the water. Although simple, they very nearly led to a fatal accident at Portsmouth, because it was necessary, in order to obtain a goal, for a team to press down in full force with one of the players holding the ball, the rest of his team round closing him so as to prevent the ball being secured by the opposing side. The ball was not allowed to be thrown, the players having to swim with it in their hands, or push it in front of them. The occasion on which Mr. J. L. Mayger —now the President of the Midland Counties Swimming Association and a well-known Rugby footballer—nearly lost his life was in the second match between England and Birmingham Leander. A fierce struggle took place near the Leander goal, which was a heavy pontoon moored against the side of a gun-boat. The tide was flowing in that direction, and Mr. Mayger, who was playing for England, was in a scrimmage pushed beneath the surface and under the pontoon. The rest of the swimmers, in their frantic endeavours to gain a goal, prevented him from getting clear. It was only when nearly insensible that his rescue was effected.

In the meantime, an attempt had been made by Mr. W. Henry to induce the English Association, then styled the Swimming Association of Great Britain, to recognise the game, and to formulate a set of rules for general use among clubs, as certain individual clubs were making rules of their own. No support was accorded to the proposition, and, as a matter of fact, only the proposer and seconder voted in favour of it. The Midlanders were, however, keen on the subject, and on May 20, 1884, a meeting of the clubs in the district was held at Burton-on-Trent, and a resolution was adopted to the effect that a Midland Counties Swimming and Aquatic Football Association be formed, the chief object being the promotion of the game of water-polo in the Midlands. This decided action induced the Swimming Association of Great Britain to reconsider their determination, and in 1885 they passed the following set of rules, and recognised the game as being under their jurisdiction :

1. Each side shall be represented by not less than six players.
2. Each side shall wear caps of a distinctive colour. The width of goal to be 10 feet, marked by flags. The ball to be not less than 8 inches in diameter.
3. The duration of the game not to exceed twenty minutes ; one minute allowed at half-time to change ends.
4. The captains shall agree or toss for choice of goals.
5. Each side shall appoint an umpire ; a referee shall also be appointed. The decision of the umpires in all questions of fact to be final ; but in the case of the umpires disagreeing, then an appeal shall be made to the referee, whose decision shall be final ; the referee shall also act as time-keeper.
6. The players shall enter the water and place themselves in line at their respective goals. A player leaving the water shall take no further part in the game.
7. The referee shall stand in a line with the centre of the course, and, after ascertaining that the captains are ready, shall give the word ' Go ! ' at the same time throwing the ball into the centre.
8. The umpires shall take their stand at each end of the course and follow the game silently ; a goal or foul to be declared by whistle.
9. The ball may be passed from one player to another, and carried either on or below the surface.
10. A goal to be obtained only by the ball being taken up by hand and fairly placed on the goal line, which may be the end of a bath, floating-stage, pole, or plank.
11. No player to interfere with the goal-keeper, or hold his opponents in any way, unless they are in possession of the ball or touching it.
12. All players must stop in their places directly the whistle is sounded by either of the umpires.
13. When the ball by any chance shall go out of play, it shal be thrown in a straight line into the middle of the course, by the referee, from the place where it went out. A player throwing the ball over his own goal-line shall concede a corner thrown to his

opponents ; but if the attacking party throw the ball over, the goal-keeper shall return the ball in a direct line from where it went out.

14. No player shall be placed in his opponents' goal.

15. In case of a foul (such as Rule 11), the opponents to have a free throw from the place where the ball is at the time the foul occurred.

The Midland rules at that time were almost similar, but for the purposes of comparison, as well as a record, they are here given :

1. Each side shall be represented by eight players.

2. The duration of a game shall be twenty minutes.

3. The sides shall be distinguished by the players wearing red and white caps respectively, and each side shall have two flags to correspond with their colours, which shall be fixed at the end of the bath. The width of the goal to be 12 feet ; size of ball 9 inches in diameter.

4. The captains shall agree or toss for choice of goals.

5. Each side shall appoint an umpire. A referee shall also be appointed by the Association, whose decision in case of dispute shall be final.

6. At the commencement of play the referee shall stand at the centre of the side of the bath, he shall then blow his whistle to signify to the captains to get ready, and, after ascertaining that the captains are ready, he shall give the word 'Go !' at the same time throwing the ball into the centre of the bath. The umpires must take their stand, one at each end of the bath, and shall follow the course of the game silently, goal or foul to be declared by whistle. Any time occupied in dispute (not exceeding five minutes) shall be added to the length of the game.

7. All players shall enter the water immediately at the commencement of the game, and remain in the water.

8. No player shall be allowed to hold an opponent, unless such opponent shall be in possession of the ball (touching it in any way). In case of any player infringing this or the preceding rules, a foul shall be at once given against his side, and his opponents shall be allowed a free throw from the place where the foul shall have occurred.

9. A goal shall be obtained by the ball being taken up by the hand and fairly 'placed' on the path at the end of the bath between

the flags. Where this is not practicable, the ball must be 'placed' against the end.

10. When the ball by any chance shall go out of play over the side of the bath, the same shall be thrown in a straight line by a player of the opposite side, from the place where it went out. A player throwing the ball over his own goal-line shall concede a corner throw to his opponents; but if the attacking party throw the ball over, the goal-keeper (or one of the opposite side) shall return the ball in a direct line from where it went out. No player may be 'placed' in his opponents' goal.

11. The teams shall change ends at half-time.

12. Any of the foregoing rules may be altered or amended, or new rules made, by the Midland Counties Association, at a meeting specially convened to consider and decide the same.

Various alterations were from time to time made until the Midlanders, like the Scotch clubs, adopted goal-posts, when their play at once improved, and the winning of a game began to depend more on the skill of the team than its combined brute force. The Midland goal-posts were only a few inches high, just sufficient to allow of the ball being put through.

While the English clubs had been gradually improving their system of play, the Scotch clubs had not been idle, and upon the formation of the Associated Swimming Clubs of Glasgow (now practically the western local centre of the Scottish Amateur Swimming Association), a committee was appointed to draft a set of rules for the proper conduct of the game, and a cup was presented for competition amongst the affiliated clubs. This contest was first decided in 1886, and as none other of its character was held in Scotland, it was to all intents and purposes the Scottish aquatic football championship. The first team to win the cup was that representing the old West of Scotland Club, who beat South Side in the final tie by one goal to love, the winning team consisting of W. Clark, captain, Stanley Priestley, J. Stevenson, G. S. Bryson, F. Williamson, J. Dickie, and A. Cooper, goal. The games were played under the following official rules of the Glasgow organisation :

1. The play to last fourteen minutes, with teams of seven a-side. Teams to change ends at half-time.

2. The teams shall be distinguished by the players wearing caps of different colours. Goal-posts to be 7 feet wide, 6 feet high from

WATER-POLO—SCOTCH STYLE

the surface of the water, and fixed 2 feet 6 inches from end of pond. The ball to be 26½ and not more than 28½ inches in circumference.

3. The captains shall agree or toss for choice of ends. Each side shall appoint an umpire, and a referee shall be appointed by

mutual agreement, whose decision in all cases of dispute shall be final.

4. At the commencement of the play the referee shall stand at the centre of the side of the bath, and shall then blow a whistle to signify to the captains to get ready, and after ascertaining that they are ready, he shall give the word to go, at the same time throwing the ball into the centre of the bath.

5. All players, with the exception of goal-keeper, shall enter the water immediately at the commencement of the game, and remain in the water while the ball is in play.

6. No player shall be allowed to duck an opponent unless such opponent shall be in possession of the ball ; no holding or pulling back of any opponent, nor (with the exception of goal-keeper) playing the ball with both hands.

7. A goal shall only be scored when the ball has been thrown or placed between the goal posts under the bar. Fouls to be declared by whistle ; goals, half-time, and time to be declared by bell.

8. No player (with exception of goal-keeper) shall be allowed to stand on bottom of bath while playing the ball.

9. A goal-keeper throwing the ball past the centre of the pond shall concede a free throw to his opponents. The free throw to be taken from the centre of either side of the bath.

10. Should the opposing team throw the ball over the end of the bath, the goal-keeper shall have a free throw from goal ; but should the defending team do so, they shall concede a corner throw.

11. No player shall be allowed to play the ball while holding on by the rail.

12. Any infringement of Rule 6, 8, or 11 shall be considered a foul. In the event of a foul being declared against any player, his opponents shall be allowed a free throw in any direction, from the side of the bath nearest to where the foul shall have occurred. A goal shall not be scored from a free throw, unless the ball has touched another player before going between the goal-posts. When a goal has been scored, the time from the scoring of the goal to the re-starting of the game, or any time lost in dispute, shall be added to the game.

Very little progress was made until the end of 1887, as the English governing body was, during the years 1884-5 and 6, engaged in perpetual wrangles as to the meaning of the amateur definition, but early in 1888 a committee was appointed, consisting of Mr. T. Young (Richmond), Mr. H. G. Hackett (Pacific), and the authors of the present volume, to revise the laws and compile a set of conditions for water-polo championships. Their report, presented in April 1888, was unanimously adopted. The new laws provided that goalposts ·8 feet wide, with a crossbar 6 feet above the surface of the water, and fixed at least one foot from the end of the bath, should be used, and that the player should be actually swimming when passing or playing the ball. For the first English championship the entries were not numerous, but this was only to be expected, as the expenses of travelling had to be borne by the individual players, who, in most cases, were mere youths, not overburdened with cash. Since then the institution of the county and district competitions has tended still further to diminish the number of clubs anxious to compete for championship honours ; but, undoubtedly, the question of expense is an effectual deterrent with many. Swimming cannot, by reason of the lack of accommodation for spectators at baths, be made to pay sufficiently well to defray the cost of visiting teams travelling long distances, and the burden therefore falls upon the clubs who happen to be unsuccessful in the draw for choice of venue.

After the decision of the preliminary rounds the Otter, Tadpole, and Nautilus (London), and the Burton-on-Trent Amateur Clubs were left in the semi-final round. Nautilus were defeated by Burton by one goal to *nil*, and as the Tadpoles scratched, the famous Otter and the crack Midland combination were left in for the final. They met at the Lambeth Baths, the game ending in an easy win for the Midlanders.

These games were very carefully watched, and the new style of play freely criticised. As an immediate result, a committee of experts was appointed to revise the laws, as it was generally conceded that some of the conditions imposed were absurd, as well as being capable of lending themselves to two or three different constructions. A voluminous correspondence was carried on between all the important clubs and organisations in the kingdom, with the result that the following rules were eventually adopted :

1. *Ball.*—The ball to be an Association football (No. 3), and to be not less than 8 nor more than 9 inches in diameter. The ball to be furnished by the home team.

2. *Goals.*—The width of the goals to be 10 feet, the crossbar to be 3 feet above the surface of the water in the deep end of the bath, and 5 feet in the shallow end. If in deep water (i.e. exceeding 5 feet in depth) both crossbars to be 3 feet above the surface. The posts to be fixed at least 1 foot from the end of the bath. The distance between the goals shall not exceed 30 yards, nor be less than 20 yards. The goal-posts to be furnished by the home team.

3. *Depth.*—The water shall not be shallower than 3 feet.

4. *Teams.*—Each side should consist of not less than 7 players, who shall wear caps of distinctive colour, and drawers or costumes.

5. *Time.*—The duration of the match should be 20 minutes— 10 minutes each way. Three minutes to be allowed at half-time for change of ends. Time occupied by disputes shall not be reckoned as in the time of play.

6. *Captains.*—The captains shall be playing members of the teams they represent ; they shall agree upon all preliminaries, and shall toss for choice of ends. If they are unable to agree upon any point, the referees shall decide for them.

7. *Officials.*—The officials shall consist of a referee (assisted by a timekeeper) and two goal judges.

8. *Referee.*—The referee's duties shall be to start the game, to stop all unfair play, to decide upon all fouls, and to see that these rules are properly carried out. He may proclaim a foul without its being claimed by any of the competitors. The referee's decision is final (note Rule 13 Championship Conditions).

9. *Goal Judges.*—The goal judges shall stand at each end of the bath, and shall decide upon the scoring of goals at their respective ends only, and shall denote a goal by means of a flag. They shall not change ends.

10. *Declaring Fouls.*—The referee shall declare a foul by blowing a whistle, upon which the competitors shall remain in their

respective positions until the colours of the side are exhibited to which the free throw is awarded.

11. *Fouls.*—It shall be a foul—

(*a*) To touch the ball with both hands at the same time (goal-keeper exempted from this rule).

(*b*) To touch the ball, interfere with an opponent, or take any part in the game whilst standing on the bottom of the bath ; the goal-keeper exempted.

(*c*) To hold the rail or side of the bath during any part of game, unless for the purpose of resting.

(*d*) To interfere with an opponent unless he is playing or holding the ball.

(*e*) To carry the ball under the arm.

12. *Penalties.*—The penalty for each foul shall be a free throw to the opposing side from the place where the foul occurred. A goal cannot be scored from a free throw unless the ball has touched at least one other player.

13. *Wilful Fouls.*—If in the opinion of the referee a player commits a wilful foul, he shall be cautioned for the first offence, and for the second the referee shall have power to order him out of the water until a goal has been scored.

14. *Goal-keeper.*—The goal-keeper may stand to defend his goal, but when standing he must not throw the ball beyond half distance ; the penalty for doing this shall be a free throw to the opposing side from the half-distance. Goal-keeper is exempt from clauses (*a*) and (*b*) in Rule 11, and he may be treated as any other player when in possession of the ball.

15. *Scoring.*—A goal shall be scored by the ball passing between the goal-posts and under the crossbar.

16. *Leaving the Water.*—A player leaving the water in which the match is being played, except at half-time, shall not re-enter it until a goal has been scored, or until half-time.

17. *Starting.*—The players shall enter the water, and place themselves in a line with their respective goals. The referee shall stand in a line with the centre of the course, and, having ascertained that the captains are ready, shall give the word 'Go,' at the same time throwing the ball into the water at the centre.

18. *Out of Play.*—When the ball shall go out of play, it shall be thrown by the referee into the middle of the course, in a straight line from where it went out.

19. *Goal-Line and Corner Throws.*—A player throwing the ball

over his own goal-line shall concede a free corner throw to his opponents ; but if the attacking side throw the ball over, it shall be a free throw to their opponents.

20. *No Player to be placed in Opponents' Goal.*—No player to be placed in his opponents' goal, or behind the goal-keeper while the ball is in front of the goal-keeper. Infringement of this rule is a wilful foul.

The height of the goal-posts was decreased, especially in the deep end, and the width of goals increased. The office of umpire was abolished, and that of goal judge substituted, whilst the referee was granted further and far more stringent power in dealing with the players than heretofore. Goal-keepers were prohibited from throwing the ball more than half the length of the bath when standing, and carrying the ball under the arm was disallowed.

Then followed a wonderful development in the game, more especially in the South, primarily due to the formation of the London Water-Polo League, a body whose sole object is to advance the game in every possible way. It has no legislative powers, and is affiliated to the Amateur Swimming Association.

A meeting of London clubs was called in 1889 by Mr. A. Sinclair, and, although but sparsely attended, it was determined to found a League for London and district, the convener of the meeting acting as hon. secretary for the three succeeding seasons. The promoters felt quite satisfied that the matter would be properly taken up, but they were more than surprised to find that when the entries for the first competition closed no fewer than twenty-one clubs had affiliated. The competition was not carried out on the League principle, but by the ordinary method. Nautilus beat Otter in the final tie by two goals to *nil*. The work of the League was not by any means confined to the mere holding of a competition. It drew up a set of instructions for referees, arranged inter-town matches, and, what is more important than all, started the now popular county games.

The first county match under its auspices—Middlesex *v.*

Surrey—was played at the annual gala of the Tadpole Club, held at Kensington on September 18, 1889, Middlesex winning by five goals to love. Through the League, a much better feeling than had previously existed was engendered among metropolitan swimming clubs, and the game was taken up strongly in the southern counties. This caused frequent discussions among players as to the different styles of play then in vogue in England, and in March 1890, at the annual general meeting of the Midland Counties' Association, a body whose membership was smaller than that of the League, the old Midland aquatic polo rules were discarded, and those framed by the A.S.A. adopted. As the Northern Association had, soon after its formation, accepted the National rules, and thereby abolished several local styles of play, the desired consummation—one system of play for the whole of the clubs in England—was arrived at.

As may be naturally imagined, the Scotch clubs had not been idle. They had gradually improved their rules, making the game more scientific and less rough ; but, although the majority simply played under one set of conditions, the inventive Edinburgh League, and one or two similar organisations, made local alterations. The official rules were the following :

1. The play to last 14 minutes, with teams of 7 aside. Teams to change ends at half-time.

2. The teams shall be distinguished by the players wearing caps of different colours. Goal-posts to be 7 feet wide, 6 feet high from the surface of the water, and fixed 2 feet 6 inches from the end of pond. The ball to be 26½ and not more than 28½ inches in circumference.

3. The captains shall agree or toss for choice of ends.

4. Each side shall appoint an umpire, and a referee shall be appointed by mutual agreement, whose decisions in all cases of dispute shall be final.

5. At the commencement of the play the referee shall stand at the centre of the side of the bath, and shall then blow a whistle to signify to the captains to get ready, and after ascertaining that they are ready he shall give the word 'Go,' at the same time throwing the ball into the centre of the bath.

6. All players, with the exception of goal-keeper, shall enter the water immediately at the commencement of the game, and remain in the water while the ball is in play.

7. No player shall be allowed to duck an opponent unless such opponent shall be in possession of the ball ; no holding or pulling back of any opponent, nor (with the exception of goal-keeper) playing the ball with both hands.

8. A goal shall only be scored when the ball has been thrown or placed between the goal-posts under the bar.

9. Fouls to be declared by whistle ; goals, half-time, and time to be declared by bell.

10. No player, with the exception of goal-keeper, shall be allowed to stand on bottom of bath while playing the ball.

11. A goal-keeper throwing the ball past the centre of the pond shall concede a free throw to his opponents. The free throw to be taken from the centre of either side of the bath.

12. Should the opposing team throw the ball over the end of the bath, the goal-keeper shall have a free throw from goal ; but should the defending team do so, they shall concede a corner throw.

13. No player shall be allowed to play the ball while holding on by the rail.

14. Any infringement of Rules 7, 10, and 13 shall be considered a foul. In the event of a foul being declared against any player, his opponents shall be allowed a free throw in any direction from where the foul took place. A goal shall not be scored from a free throw unless the ball has touched another player before going between the goal-posts. When a goal has been scored, the time from the scoring of the goal to the re-starting of the game, or any time lost in dispute, shall be added to the game.

For open water the rules as to goals and goal-keeper were the same as in England.

The Edinburgh League began active work in December 1890, and its matches were carried out with success right through the succeeding winter. All its games were conducted after the racing was over for the year, as the accommodation in Edinburgh was then, and is now at the time of writing, but meagre. Their rules differed somewhat from those adopted by the Scottish Association, the principal differences being as follows :—When 'a goal was scored, instead of lining up at their respective ends, the teams took up their positions, the forward lines being three feet from the centre of the pond, and when starting the ball the centre forward of the team against whom the goal had been scored had the throw-off, but had to pass to either wing, and not back. Ten clubs took part in the first competition, but this number was decreased to eight in the second year.

The Irish clubs in Dublin and Belfast had two different sets. That at Belfast was an amalgamation of the English and Scotch rules, but those adopted by the Sandycove and Black-rock Clubs were totally different, the swimmers not being allowed to throw the ball at goal, but being required to place it between two painted marks. At the start the players took up their positions, and the ball was hit off from the centre by the side losing the toss for choice of ends.

In the year 1890 the London League greatly extended its sphere of action, and arranged matches between Middlesex and Surrey, Kent, Sussex, and Hants. This was the direct cause of the formation of county associations, the rise and progress of which will be dealt with later.

The League was also desirous of playing Glasgow, and instructed its secretary to try and arrange the meeting. Through error application was made to the central body of the Scottish Swimming Association instead of to its Western local centre. The Scotch council were entirely in accord with the movement, but wanted an international rather than an inter-town match. As a result, the first international match between England and Scotland was arranged. It was played at Kensington Baths on July 28, 1890, the teams being as follows : —

*England.*—F. Browne (Burton-on-Trent), goal ; W. G. Carrey (Amateur), and H. F. Clark (Stroud Green), backs ; J. F. Genders (Nautilus), half-back ; J. Finegan (Liverpool Sefton), W. Henry (Zephyr), and J. L. Mayger (Burton-on-Trent), captain, forwards.

*Scotland.*—C. W. Donald (Edinburgh University), goal ;

G. S. Bryson (Dennistoun), and S. D. Cawood (Victoria), backs ; A. Strauss (Southern), captain, half-back ; J. Bissland (Leander), A. Whyte (Victoria), and S. Capie (Dennistoun), forwards.

The English rules were used, but the Scotchmen ably demonstrated that their style of play was the better. They did not indulge in the ducking tactics so common with their opponents, and were far smarter in playing the ball. It was evident that the English 'ducking' rule was not stringent enough, and that the Scotch game was far superior as an exhibition of scientific and fast play. It was very often impossible for a player, no matter how fairly he might wish to act, to prevent fouling his opponent, because he could not always tell whether his opponent had the ball in his possession or not. The Scotchmen did not trouble about this in the least, but simply went for the ball, avoiding ducking in every instance. Another difficulty was the continued holding of a player after the ball had left his possession. When a player legally tackled took the ball under the water, it very often happened that in the succeeding struggle the ball was released, but that the tackler, not knowing this, still held on, and as a consequence had a foul awarded against him. In the shallow end of the bath the Englishmen repeatedly infringed the rule prohibiting standing when playing. It is, of course, hard to avoid standing in the shallow end of a bath, but the leaping from the bottom at the ball was so palpable an infringement that the onlookers quickly acknowledged that the Scotch game was better than that in vogue in England. From this it will be seen that, although England had made far more rapid strides than the sister country in the promulgation of the pastime, the Scotchmen had developed and improved their rules to such an extent as to make their passing and swimming powers far superior to that of the best combination England could bring together. The Englishmen were far heavier and speedier than their opponents, but were sadly lacking in skill and strategy. They suffered defeat by four goals to *nil*.

The English championship of 1890 again obtained a meagre entry, but the pick of the English clubs were engaged. As already mentioned, Burton won in 1888, the year of the institution of the contest, and as in the succeeding year they again won, beating Hanley in the first round by two goals to love, Nautilus in the semi-final by three goals to love, and Amateur in the final by two goals to love, their victory for the third successive year was confidently expected. They, however, suffered defeat in the final at Birmingham, Hanley winning by six goals to love. The absence of some of their best players may have been the cause of such a crushing defeat, but it was the opinion of good judges that Hanley would have won in any case.

The Manchester League was formed in March of this year, the A.S.A. rules being at once adopted as those to be used by the clubs engaged in its competitions. Mr. Herbert Dean was elected secretary, and in a very short time the League was at work. The system during the first year was to play one match against each other club entered, the choice of bath being drawn for. Mayfield, Gorton, Osborne, Swan, Leaf Street, Chalmers, Tyldesley, Stalybridge, Oldham Seal, and Stretford were the clubs that constituted the League, but the Swan Club afterwards withdrew, because the League ruled against them over a protest and the Y.M.C.A. thereupon undertook to play all their matches. The Mayfield Club won the League championship after being victorious in every game, and scoring eighty-five goals as against seven scored by their opponents. England again suffered a reverse in the International match, which was played at Glasgow in October 1891, under the rules of the Scotch Association ; but the defeat served a good purpose in the interests of the pastime, as the officials of both bodies then attempted to assimilate the two codes, and in April of the following year, 1892, an international conference was held at Liverpool, the delegates being G. H. Barker (Liverpool), chairman, A. Thomson (Manchester), H. Thomsett (Leicester), A. J. Foster (Birmingham), and the writers as representing England,

Loudoun Hamilton (Glasgow), A. Graham (Glasgow), and J. Lamb (Edinburgh League), representing Scotland. Prior to the meeting of the conference, the Midland, Northern, and Southern Associations had agreed to a revised set of rules, and these were submitted to the meeting at Liverpool. The Scotch style of play was adopted almost in its entirety, as well as their time-keeping rule, aimed at the prevention of a system of winning by delay, which had become too common in England. The great fight was over the goal-posts, but after a long discussion those in vogue in England were accepted by the International Board on a division. The opposition came from the Scotch Association, under whose rules goal-keepers stood on the side of the bath to defend their goals, and as the substitution of the English rule entirely altered the play of their men, it was natural that the subject should occasion prolonged argument. The English delegates ably maintained that in a swimming game the players should be swimming, and not standing on the side of the bath. In the course of the next few months the recommendations of the International Board were considered by the governing associations, and unanimously accepted by them. The assimilated code was as follows :

### AMATEUR SWIMMING ASSOCIATION WATER-POLO RULES
#### REVISED 1892

1. *Ball.*—The ball to be an Association football, fully inflated, and to be not less than 26$\frac{1}{2}$ inches nor more than 28$\frac{1}{2}$ inches in circumference. The ball shall be furnished by the home team, and no oil, grease, or other objectionable substance shall be placed on it.

2. *Goals.*—The width of the goals to be 10 feet, the crossbar to be 3 feet above the surface when the water is 5 feet or over in depth, and to be 8 feet from the bottom when the water is less than 5 feet in depth. The goal-posts to be furnished by the home team.

3. *Field of Play.*—The distance between the goals shall not exceed 30 yards nor be less than 19 yards, the width shall not be

more than 20 yards, and the goal-posts shall be fixed at least one foot from the end of the bath or any obstruction.

4. *Depth.*—The water shall not be shallower than 3 feet.

5. *Time.*—The duration of the match shall be 14 minutes, 7 minutes each way. Three minutes to be allowed at half time for change of ends. When a goal has been scored, the time from the scoring of the goal to the re-starting of the game, or time occupied by disputes or fouls, shall not be reckoned as in the time of play.

6. *Officials.*—The officials shall consist of a referee, time-keeper, and two goal-scorers.

7. *Referee.*—The referee's duties shall be to start the game, stop all unfair play, decide in all cases of dispute, declare fouls, goals, half-time, and time, and see that these rules are properly carried out. He may proclaim a foul without its being claimed by any of the competitors, and shall decide upon and declare all goals, whether signified or not. The referee's decison is final.

8. *Goal-Scorers.*—The goal-scorers shall stand at the side near each goal, and when they consider that the ball has passed through the goal, at their respective ends only, they shall signify the same to the referee by means of a flag. They shall not change ends, and shall keep the score of goals of each team at their respective ends.

9. *Teams.*—Each side shall consist of not more than seven players, who shall wear caps of distinctive colour, and drawers or costumes. In baths no grease, oil, or other objectional substance shall be rubbed on the body.

10. *Captains.*—The captains shall be playing members of the teams they represent; they shall agree upon all preliminaries, and shall toss for choice of ends. If they are unable to agree upon any point, the referee shall decide for them.

11. *Starting.* — The players shall enter the water and place themselves in a line with their respective goals. The referee shall stand in a line with the centre of the course, and, having ascertained that the captains are ready, shall give the word 'Go,' and immediately throw the ball into the water at the centre. A goal shall not be scored after starting or re-starting until the ball has touched more than one player.

12. *Scoring.*—A goal shall be scored by the entire ball passing beyond the goal-posts and under the crossbar.

13. *Fouls.*—It shall be a foul—

(*a*) To touch the ball with both hands at the same time.

(*b*) To hold the rail or side during any part of the game.

(*c*) To stand on or touch the bottom during any part of the game, unless for the purpose of resting.

(*d*) To duck an opponent unless he is holding the ball. or to retain possession of the ball when ducked.

(*e*) To jump from the bottom or push from the side (except at starting or re-starting) in order to play the ball or duck an opponent.

(*f*) To hold, pull back, or push off from an opponent.

(*g*) To turn on the back and kick at an opponent.

14. *Penalties.*—The penalty for each foul shall be a free throw to the opposing side from the place where the foul occurred. A goal cannot be scored from a free throw unless the ball has touched at least one other player.

15.—*Wilful Fouls.*—If, in the opinion of the referee, a player commits an' ordinary foul wilfully, he shall be cautioned for the first offence, and for the second the referee shall have the power to order him out of the water until a goal has been scored. It shall be a wilful foul to start before the word ' Go,' to deliberately waste time, or for a player to take up a position within a yard of his opponents' goal.

16. *Declaring Fouls.*—The referee shall declare a foul by blowing a whistle and exhibiting the colour of the side to which the free throw is awarded, whose captain may appoint any player to take the throw from where the foul occurred. The other players shall remain in their respective positions from the blowing of the whistle until the ball has left the hand of the player taking the throw.

17. *Goal-keepers.*—The goal-keeper may stand to defend his goal, and must not throw the ball beyond half-distance ; the penalty for doing so shall be a free throw to the opposing side from half-distance at either side of the field of play. Goal-keeper is exempt from clauses (*a*), (*c*), and (*e*) in Rule 13, and he may be treated as any other player when in possession of the ball.

18. *Goal-line and Corner Throws.*—A player throwing the ball over his own goal-line shall concede a free corner throw to his opponents, but if the attacking side throw the ball over, it shall be a free throw to their opponents' goal-keeper.

19. *Out of Play.*—Should a player send the ball out of the field of play at either side, it shall be thrown in any direction from where it went out by one of the opposing side, and shall be considered a free throw.

20. *Declaring Goals, Time, &c.*—The referee shall declare half-time and time by whistle ; goals by bell.

21. *Leaving the Water.*—A player leaving the water, or sitting, or standing on the steps, or on the side of the bath in which the match is being played, except at half-time or by permission of the referee, shall not re-enter it until a goal has been scored, or until half-time. Should a player leave the water, he can only re-enter it at his own goal-line.

Next in importance to the work of the various Leagues comes that of the county associations, whose delegates have now become a powerful factor in water-polo circles. Undoubtedly the most energetic has been the Surrey County Association, which was formed in 1890, under the presidency of J. F. Genders. It at once took the lead in activity among the other counties. The affairs of the Association are conducted by a committee, elected annually by the delegates of the affiliated clubs, and individual members of the Association. Besides arranging matches with the other counties and the Universities, a large number of matches are played annually in different districts in the county, for which teams are nominated by the Association. This is for the purpose of giving the officials an opportunity of finding out and giving practice to young and comparatively unknown players.

In addition to these matches, an inter-club competition, open to all amateur clubs in the county, is carried out each year on the League principle, each club playing the others.

The Association does not confine itself merely to the propagation of water-polo, but interests itself on behalf of swimming and swimming clubs in the county, using its efforts to get schools to take a greater interest in swimming and water-polo, and also advocating the adoption of the Public Baths and Washhouses Acts in suitable districts.

The first county match played by Kent was one arranged by the London League at Tunbridge Wells, the opposing county being Middlesex. It was played on July 26, 1890, the home county, which was almost entirely composed of members of the Tunbridge Wells Cygnus Club, winning by four goals to three. This success caused the honorary secretary of the Cygnus Club to endeavour to form a county association ; but the Kentish clubs did not respond very readily, and for another season the Cygnets had to carry on the work almost unaided, but they were so successful that at the end of the season the other clubs rallied round, and the Kent County Water-Polo Association was established, E. J. Plumbridge (Tunbridge Wells) being captain. Since its formation it has done good work, and large crowds have gathered at Tunbridge Wells to witness its matches. Many new players have been unearthed by means of a challenge shield competition for affiliated clubs, won the first year by Tunbridge Wells ; and there is reason to believe that, although the officials have greater difficulties to contend with in raising teams than the really metropolitan counties, whose men are always at hand, Kent will make and maintain a leading place in county water-polo.

Of Sussex there is little to be said. They formed a county association in 1891, lost all their matches, and with their losses apparently all heart.

The Middlesex County Water-Polo Association was started in April 1891. Its players were then at the head of the counties, and have remained so until the present time. · Like the Surrey Association, it arranges matches with Kent, Hants, and Surrey regularly, but has not met the Universities. Its first captain was W. Henry, of the Zephyr Club, and A. Hudson, Amateur, acted as secretary. During its first season as a properly constituted county association its representatives scored 36 goals, as against 6 obtained by their opponents; but in 1892 this goal record was lowered considerably, owing to improvement in the play of the other counties. Surrey almost grasped the lead from them, but an unlucky defeat by Hants robbed them of the honour. By affiliating to the London League, it was granted a direct seat on the executive of that body ; and as a like privilege was accorded to Surrey County, the League committee has become an organisation of experts. They have no legislative power, and are compelled to take all questions as to alterations of rules to the A.S.A., but their opinions hold a great weight in the South, and it may be safely assumed that anything brought forward by them represents the feeling of a large section of Southern water-polo players.

The rise of water-polo in Hampshire was for a time retarded by the absence of properly constructed swimming-baths. As previously stated, a ball game in the open sea was played off the old pier at Bournemouth as long back as 1876, but it was not until 1891—fifteen years later—that the Hampshire Water-Polo Association was formed, and by a most curious coincidence both events took place on the same date—July 13. The town of Bournemouth is situated on one of the most exposed portions of the Hampshire mainland coast-line, so that there has never been much inducement or incentive to the game there. For some reason or other, a long break of nearly nine years elapsed before anything further was heard of 'aquatic hand-ball' on this part of the coast. In 1885 it was revived by members of the Bournemouth Amateur Rowing Club, who had added a swimming section to the club, and occasional games were carried out in the sea at a depth varying from eight to thirty feet of water, the ball used being a large india-rubber one, such as could be bought in a toyshop. A rival rowing-club was about then started at Boscombe, an east suburb of the town, and W. Pickford, captain of the Bournemouth Club swimming section, and H. Bazalgette, captain of the Boscombe Club, son of the late Sir Joseph Bazalgette, the eminent engineer, drew up a code of regulations. Considering that none of the local swimmers had any knowledge that the game was being played in any other part of the country, and were almost under the impression that they were making a new game entirely, the rules agreed upon compare in a most interesting manner with the present conditions under which the game is played, and which were not generally adopted until about 1891. The regulations were that not less than six players should be on each side, that the goals should be ten yards wide, and the ball not less than eight inches in diameter. The game was to last twenty minutes, players were to start in a line with their respective goals, and any player leaving the water was to take no further part in the game. A referee and two umpires were to be appointed. The former had to start the game, having ascertained that the captains were ready, by uttering the word 'Go,' and throwing the ball into the centre. His only other duty was to act as timekeeper, and to decide between the umpires if they disagreed. The umpires were stationed at each goal, and were to declare the scoring of a goal, or a foul, by the sound of a whistle. A further stipulation prevented any player from grasping or throwing the ball, interfering with the goal-keeper, or holding an opponent in any way ; and at the sound of the whistle every player was to remain in his place without moving. A player was 'off-side' unless he had two opponents in front of him ;· the penalty for a foul was a free throw to the other side ; and when the ball went out of play the referee had to throw it into the centre of play again.

Contrasting these rules of 'hand-ball' with those under which water-polo is now played, the similarity in many instances is so great that one might almost imagine that the Amateur Swimming Association had a copy before them when they recently set to work to draft out their own revised series. Written copies of the rules were nailed up in both boathouses; but only one match took place—in 1886, when Boscombe won by one goal to *nil*. The sea was very choppy, and H W. Francis, a powerful and experienced sea-swimmer, pushed the ball in front of him for nearly thirty yards, and swam clean through the goal with it. The ball used was a grey rubber ball with an elastic mouthpiece. It was blown up to about a foot in diameter, and the nipple twisted and turned inside. After the match it was deflated, and carried away in the captain's pocket. Another match at Bournemouth Regatta was prevented by the tremendously heavy seas, though so anxious were both teams to play that they spent the best part of an hour and swamped two rowing-boats in their efforts to anchor the mark-flags. Failing in this, the whole crowd swam twice round the pier-head, tossed about like corks, and returned to shore with a puffin, or 'diver-bird,' caught by one of the players.

In March 1888 Messrs. Roberts and Milledge's salt-water swimming-bath was opened, the game—still known as 'hand-ball,' and played under the original rules—was revived in real earnest, and a series of matches between the Bournemouth Amateur Rowing Club, the Boscombe Rowing Club, the Bournemouth Y.M.C.A., the Bournemouth Gymnasium, and a scratch 'town' team were played. In April the amended rules, drawn up by the Amateur Swimming Association, at last reached Bournemouth, and instead of placing the goals at the ends of the bath, a foot above the surface, and starting the game by all diving in at the word 'Go,' the new plan was adopted. The old ball was retained, nothing being said in the rules about it. The new rules, by allowing ducking and holding, made the game much rougher than before; and a local paper, referring to a match played, said, 'The Swimming Association rules for water-polo are not at all liked by the locals, who prefer the old scientific passing game.'

The Lymington Swimming Club, thanks to the exertions of E. Helsby, H. E. S. Adams, and Alderman W. Murdoch, at that time the Mayor, was visited by Bournemouth swimmers, and the game established in their open sea-water baths. By 1889 the Bournemouth Rowing Club team had been displaced by the Y.M.C.A., but in August the same year the Bournemouth Swimming Club was formed, and absorbed all the contending local clubs into its ranks. E. J. Stidolph was the hon. sec., but was afterwards succeeded by R. Reid, and W. Pickford, who has supplied us with many items of interest relating to the history of the game in his district, was appointed captain.

The game now advanced rapidly, and in the summer of 1890 a visit was made to Portsmouth, where, off the Club's landing-stage, on the Southsea beach, the Bournemouth team won easily by eight goals to *nil*. The local team had scarcely an idea of the game ; and in the subsequent match, Hants *v.* Middlesex, at the Portsmouth S. C. annual festival, the Bournemouth contingent were the backbone of the team, which was only beaten by three goals to one. The tactics and play of the more advanced Middlesex men made a deep impression, and gave the locals a better idea of the game. These matches created a good deal of interest, and the game was taken up at Southampton, where there was then only a large, open, circular sea-water bath. In July 1891 the Southampton club, newly formed, visited Bournemouth, and were easily beaten. After the match, in the course of the customary entertainment to the visiting team, the subject of a Hampshire Water-polo Association was discussed ; and a fortnight later, at a representative meeting of the Portsmouth, Southampton, Lymington, and Bournemouth clubs, the Association was formed, with R. Reid as hon. sec., and H. W. Fisk of Portsmouth as president. The Bournemouth Club presented the new body with a twenty-guinea challenge cup, and matches were arranged with Surrey, with whom Hampshire made a draw of three goals each at Bournemouth Baths, but were subsequently beaten at the Victoria Baths, Peckham, by six to *nil*. In connection with this match the Bournemouth team carried out their first tour, and were disastrously beaten by the Nautilus and Tunbridge Wells Swimming Clubs, but, learning by experience more scientific play, were able to run the Ravensbourne Club to a draw. On returning home they won the Hampshire Cup for the first time, easily beating Portsmouth S.C. by twelve to *nil*, and Southampton S.C. by three to *nil*.

Thanks, however, to the coaching of A. W. McMinn, an old Hanley S.C. player, who had come to reside in Southampton, that team began to make rapid progress. In the spring of 1892 the new Corporation Baths were opened there, and on that occasion the Bournemouth Club were invited to a match, which they won by five to *nil*, the Southampton men being as yet unused to bath-work. Later on, however, they had so far improved that in the first round of the Hants Cup they played two drawn games with Bournemouth, being afterwards beaten by five goals to *nil*. Lymington scratched to Portsmouth, who in turn were beaten by the Bournemouth second team by seven goals to one, and Bournemouth first again won the cup, defeating their second team in the final. This year G. Dominy undertook the duties of honorary secretary to the Association. The county match with Middlesex was lost by six goals to two, but that with Surrey was won by one goal to *nil*. Owing to the scattered character of the county, and there being only three closed swimming-baths, from twenty-five to thirty miles apart, the progress of the game in Hampshire is not likely to be very rapid. It is to be hoped, however, that, after taking such a firm root in the county, the game will continue to flourish.

The lead of the Southern counties has been followed in the North by Lancashire and Yorkshire. The former county played their first match at the end of 1892 against Notts, and defeated their opponents. They have now organised their forces, and it seems probable that before long they will make a bold bid for premier county honours. Yorkshire water-polo is principally fostered by means of an inter-club competition, which is creating great interest in the county owing to the efforts of Mr. W. J. Ruddock, an old Norwich swimmer. Leicestershire also has an association, and will probably endeavour to arrange matches with the other counties in the future. As soon as the counties formed definite associations, the question of county qualifications began to be discussed, and at the initiative of the writers, and with the approval of London League and Surrey County, the following was brought before the A.S.A. and unanimously passed :

That the qualifications required for players in county matches shall be :—Birth or twelve months' continual residence before playing; also that :

(1) No player shall be eligible to play for more than one county in any one year.

(2) Whilst qualifying by residence a player shall be eligible to play on the behalf of the county for which he last played, but in no instance must clause 1 be infringed.

This is now binding on all the county associations.

The most pleasant games of water-polo are undoubtedly those in deep open still water. So much more scope is given for skilful play that fouling is largely avoided, and the absolute necessity for swimming, or keeping afloat without aid all through the match, assists in no small degree to develop and improve the staying powers of those taking part therein. Unfortunately there are but few spaces of open water which are available or suitable for the game, and the almost total absence of them in large cities compels the various associations to conduct their championships and other competitions in ordinary covered-in baths, which are, as a rule, far too shallow for the game to be played properly. The players, taking advantage of the opportunities offered them, naturally indulge whenever possible in a rest, by standing on the bottom of the bath.

Of the open water-baths which are suitable for the game, those at Tunbridge Wells have obtained the greatest notoriety. They are admirably situated, and the natural sloping banks afford a fine view for the spectators, who can look down from them into the bath, and follow every movement in the game.

For years past the local club has striven hard to popularise water-polo, and their matches are now always attended by an enthusiastic crowd of residents. Their home-match results afford an interesting table for comparison, as against the results of their games played away. These latter, in the majority of cases, are, of course, played in ordinary town baths. At home, the Tunbridge Wells Cygnus have time and again vanquished teams who in their respective districts are considered invincible, the altered conditions under which the game is played in deep water no doubt aiding in the downfall of the visiting clubs. Many of the losing combinations have been compelled to admit that a long hard struggle in deep water, without any possible chance of rest except at half-time, is a far different thing to a swift passing game in a shallow bath, where, during one half of the match at least, an occasional rest can be taken. Further, in covered baths the water is usually tepid, and upon those swimmers whose practice is almost wholly confined to them the temperature of open water has naturally a great effect. That in itself should be sufficient proof, if it be needed, that water-polo in open water will develop those powers which

GOAL-POSTS FOR OPEN WATER

in cases of extremity and danger may be of extreme practical use to a swimmer. There are many who cannot stay long in open water, but in most instances this is merely due to habitual practice, with frequent rests, as well as short-distance racing, in heated baths.

As already stated, the play in open water is far different from that in a confined bath. The field of play is much larger, and the opportunities for making use of the swimming abilities and staying powers of a team consequently greater. The boundaries are usually marked out by means of floating buoys with flags, the goal-posts being placed at each end of the field of play. They cannot be more than thirty or less than nineteen yards apart. The width of the field of play is limited to twenty yards or less. It is always well to make the size of the field of play as large as the rules permit. For open water, a very ingenious yet easily made goal-post is used by the London League when on tour, and as it has been adopted by a number of clubs, and is light and portable, a description of its manufacture is given here.

Take two boards about 6 inches wide, 1 inch thick, and 10 feet 6 inches long, and place them parallel with each other about 6 inches apart, or else join two or three boards together. Then obtain two lengths of 3-inch battening, 2 feet 6 inches long, and fix with thumbscrews across each end of the two parallel boards on the under side. This will make a floating platform 18 inches wide, with two cross-pieces projecting 1 foot. Then to the extremity of the projecting pieces hinge two upright posts, 3 feet 3 inches long, of similar battening, and fit a thin support to the outside of each upright post and cross-piece by means of thumbscrews, as in the diagram on preceding page. To the top of the uprights fix the crossbar, also with thumbscrews. The crossbar must be as light as possible. It may be made out of a thin batten 3 inches wide, $\frac{1}{2}$ inch to $\frac{5}{8}$ inch thick, and placed against the uprights with the small edge downwards, the top being level with the top of the uprights. By this method a goal-post 10 feet wide and 3 feet high can be easily constructed, and as the whole of it may be taken to pieces in a few minutes, its advantage will be apparent to all clubs who play in open water, and who in many cases do not have goal-posts of the proper dimensions, or have to erect fresh posts for every game.

These posts can be fixed in position with bags of ballast, the ropes being fastened to each end of the goal-posts to keep them from swinging round. They should be thrown out as far as possible from each end. If a committee boat be available, it should be moored alongside the posts. When playing in the sea, particular notice should be taken as to the direction in which the tide is flowing, as the posts should be fixed athwart the tide, otherwise the play is all at one end, i.e. that towards which the tide is flowing. In baths the width of the field of play is determined by the size of the bath, varying from about 25 to 40 feet. The length must not be more than 30 yards, or less than 19 yards, the somewhat peculiar minimum being due to the fact that there are a number of baths in England only 20 yards long. The posts are fixed not less than 1 foot from each end. In the longer baths the posts in the shallow end are often brought forward, so as to get the deeper water to play in, but the game is never so satisfactory from a swimming point of view in a bath as in open water. The goal-posts are generally made now of light galvanized-iron piping, with broad shoes to rest on the bottom of the bath. When they are fixed at the end of the bath, they are held in position by means of a clip bracket one foot long, the uprights resting on the bottom, and the bracket clipping them to the rail of the bath. The crossbar is adjusted with a thumbscrew and ring. When the posts have to be placed some distance up the bath away from the end, they have to be fixed in a similar manner to a horizontal bar, the attachments being made of cord and fixed to the rail or side of bath, boxes, or gallery. Another system, and perhaps more simple than any, is one by which the posts are lowered from the roof of the bath by means of pulley cords, and, being heavy, they keep in position.

A great improvement is that adopted by Surrey County, of fixing painted wood framework in front of the posts above the water level, so as to make the goal as clear as possible for the player.

The posts should not be painted of a dark colour, but striped red and white, or some other easily recognisable combination of colours, because most games are played in artificial light, and it is difficult for the officials as well as the players to see the posts distinctly if not coloured as recommended.

Careful attention should also be given to the caps worn by players, as in many instances club colours are so much alike that it is often quite impossible for spectators to distinguish the different players in a match who may not be personally known to them. From a long experience we think it would be wise for the various Leagues and Associations to frame a rule compelling clubs in all their matches to wear either red or white caps of approved pattern.

Two or three kinds of caps are used, but the best are those as illustrated in this sketch. They are best made of turkey twill or similar cotton material, the side-flaps fitting over the ears, and the cap being laced, tied, or buttoned under the chin. They

REGULATION POLO CAP

should be fastened securely, so as to avoid the possibility of their being pulled off during the game.

In consequence of the sudden changes of front which are necessary to good play, regular practice is important. It must not consist of the mere pitching of the ball. The arrangement of friendly matches, or the selection of teams from among the members of one club, is a far more effectual method of gaining real practice and experience. A player who wishes to become an expert must devote a considerable time to the study of the niceties of the game, or else in big contests, where every man should be keenly working for the victory of his side, he will be worse than useless. During the last few years, the game of water-polo has been far more scientifically played than it was at the outset, and the various alterations of the rules which have been detailed have tended towards this end, as they have been the means of introducing combined instead of loose play. The system prevalent up to 1888 was a mere exhibition of brute strength. Passing, punting, and dribbling the ball were scarcely ever practised, and, except in the case of the leading teams, rarely attempted.

Until the first international match was played, nearly every game was fought out on individual lines ; that is to say, the members of the teams considered that their sole duty, without regard to position, was the scoring of goals ; and very often this anxiety to spoil the combination of a side led to ludicrous defeats. Yet it must not be imagined that every player or every team did this. There were some who strictly played out their games on a sound system of combination ; and it was by reason of their victories that attention was called to many anomalies in the then code of laws. When England's picked seven met the Scots for the first time, the eyes of water-polo players were opened ; for the Scots, who were nearly all lightly built men, simply made an exhibition of their opponents, who during the game could not understand or in any way checkmate the skilful passing and dribbling tactics of the victors. To the experience gained in the international match may therefore rightly be attributed the improvement in the game all round ; for though the Scots had made more rapid progress than their Southern brethren, they have also benefited largely by the innovation.

The general custom is to divide a team up as follows : Goal, two backs, half-back, centre forward, two forwards. The office of captain is, of course, a very important one. It is hardly necessary to say that he must be well versed not only in the rules of the game, but also those of the competition or competitions in which his club may at the time be contending. He should organise regular and frequent practices, take careful note of the faults or merits of each individual player, and be careful that none of them, including himself, infringes the laws, or gives cause for complaint by another club. It is his duty to instruct and advise the players on all points of the game, to show them what positions they should take up in relation to each other so that the play of each of them may be effective, and to see that they do not leave their opponents free at any time for attack or defence. No selfishness in scoring should be allowed by him, and the urgent need of good combination should be frequently pointed out. He must impress upon each member of the team that standing or walking in shallow water must be avoided, as nothing is gained thereby, because while walking or standing a foul may unwittingly be committed at a critical portion of the game, and either the whole attack or defence, as the case may be, spoilt. The team should be advised always to play the ball, and never duck an opponent unless he is unmistakably holding the ball. Quick, short passing should be practised rather than long shots, as to make a long shot effective one has to get into a certain position, and in doing so time—an all-important essential in a fast game—is lost.

The swiftness with the ball and accuracy of throw of each player should be individually tested by the captain before the man is admitted to the team. A player may have plenty of strength, but bad judgment in the use of it. Above all, absolute obedience to the captain's signs or orders must be insisted upon.

## FORWARDS

The forwards must be good swimmers who can catch a ball, quickly judge distances, pass, dribble, and shoot strongly and accurately from any portion of the field of play. One of them should take up a position either on the right or left of the opponents' goal, but outside the prescribed limit. The other should take the opposite side, but be a little farther away from the goal. Both should always be on the alert for the ball, but in place of holding it should make quick, short passes to each other or to the centre forward, the ball in all cases being passed to the side furthest away from goal, and never direct into the other's hands, unless uncovered by the opposing back. If it be passed directly to a covered player, he will almost to a surety be tackled with it; whereas, if it be passed on the outside of him, he at once gets an opportunity, if he be a fast swimmer, of clearing himself from the cover. The forwards should always hold themselves ready for a quick stroke or two, so as to clear; but this ability will come by practice. When this is acquired, the forwards will find that very often an almost free throw at goal can be obtained.

When dribbling the ball the forwards should clear on the outside and pass rapidly if likely to be tackled by an opposing player.

They should keep well up towards goal, and if the centre forward gain possession, one of the other forwards should at once take his place, because if the attempt at goal be frustrated he will then be in a position to renew the attack.

It is the duty of the forwards to keep free, as far as possible, from the opposing side, and, when a change has taken place owing to their opponents' defence play, to get back to position as quickly as possible. They should take care not to infringe the rule prohibiting a player from taking up a position within a yard of the opposing goal, and should also avoid placing themselves too far over to the side of the bath or field of play.

When engaged in attacking, if the ball be in danger of crossing the goal-line, care should be taken to avoid touching it. The opposing back should in this case be hard pressed, prevented from making a long shot, and, if possible, compelled in self-defence to concede a corner. No time should be lost in taking the corner throw, because, although the rules prohibit a change of position between the blowing of the whistle and the taking of the throw, delay allows the backs to get their bodies better balanced for a quick start, and the advantage accruing from the free throw is thereby neutralised.

## CENTRE FORWARD

Upon the centre forward devolves the task of guiding the forward play. He should be in touch with the wing forwards, and, when their chance of scoring seems more open than his, should always pass out to them. He must be utterly unselfish in his play, look well after the opposing half-back, and in a wide field of play, if possible, tire him by dribbling or punting the ball from side to side in a zigzag forward direction, and then, when in danger of being tackled, pass rapidly forward either to the nearest forward or to the one on the other side, as opportunity offers. With a centre forward, as, in fact, with all other players, a knowledge of the 'Trudgeon' stroke is invaluable. Nearly every good man now uses this or an imitation of it in water-polo, because a change of position is more rapidly secured, the speed is faster for a short distance, and the opponents can be seen. The hints given for the play of forwards apply equally to the centre forward. He should be quick and sure with the ball, a first-class swimmer, and one well able to stay through a tiring game.

## HALF-BACK

The half-back has the most onerous post in a team. With the forwards a certain amount of individual play is necessary, but a half-back must make combination the essential feature of his play. He must be ready to assist the attack, and be as much in touch with his backs as the centre forward is with the forwards. The centre forward of the opposing team is the man that he must watch, and whose attack play he must try to nullify. If he keep cool and do not rashly shoot at goal, he will prove of immense service to his side. The forwards should be well fed by him, and left to score when able. It is only by a bare chance that a half-back can score, and in good matches the attack is spoilt if the half-back, instead of passing, selfishly tries to shoot between the posts. He should be a good swimmer, well able to dribble or punt, and throw or pass with either hand under any conditions. At the starting of the game either the half-back or the centre forward should be told off by the captain according to speed—the fastest swimmer for preference—to sprint for the ball, and if he obtain possession to pass it back. If the centre forward be allotted this duty, he should pass to the half-back and then swim on to his position, whilst the wing forwards are also taking up their places. If the half-back has to go for the ball, he should pass to his backs and return to his proper place, which is some two or three yards in advance of the backs. As soon as the backs receive the ball, it should be held until the forwards are up in position, and then passed to them. Upon the play of the half-back greatly depends the success of the team, and a clear-headed, sure, and swift swimmer should be appointed to fill this post. He must by practice learn to know instinctively the place of every man in the team, must never stand, and always be ready to accept a pass, no matter how fast it may come.

## BACKS

The backs should take up a position near to their opponents' forwards in order to prevent them from scoring, but they should never allow them to be between them and their own goal. They must closely watch them, and be ever ready to move rapidly when danger threatens. It is usual to appoint the heaviest men in the team as backs, but judgment must of course be used as to their capabilities ; because it is better to have a strong defence and a weak attack than a weak defence and a strong attack. This is particularly noticeable when the game is played in open water. The backs are very often called upon to save under very difficult circumstances, as when hard pressed by speedier swimmers than themselves, and thus it is very necessary that they should keep close watch of their opponents, at the same refraining from holding or impeding them. They should be smart and tactical, be alive to the necessity of giving away a corner, or of passing to their goal-keeper when the goal is in danger. They must also be capable of passing to one another, or else forward to the half-back. There must be no hesitation in their work. They should never leave their place after passing, or allow the opposing forwards to get away from them. Their passes should be short, so that the half-back may reach them easily. They may pass to their forwards if opportunity occurs for obtaining a deliberate and strong shot. The work of the half-back and backs should be so regular and combined that the forwards may place confidence in them. This will prevent the latter from leaving their own .positions to assist in the defence.

### GOAL-KEEPER

The position of goal-keeper is not eagerly sought after, and in many instances the post is given to a wretched swimmer. It is not difficult to find the reason of this. The goal-keeper has the cold and thankless task of keeping in one place during the game, and cannot exercise himself by swimming. Men who can swim well are chary of having thrown upon them the arduous task of guarding the goal mouth, which is made doubly difficult if the team lack combination. Notwithstanding this a good swimmer should be appointed, and one well able to float and support himself with the legs. To properly defend a goal requires skill, rapidity of action, keen judgment, quick and sure catching, and the ability to throw or punch out imme- diately the ball comes, in a direction which will be of service to the side. In all practice the goal-keeper should be careful to avoid sending the ball past the centre of the bath or bringing it under the crossbar when throwing. If half a dozen forwards are put on for shooting practice, each with a ball, the goal-keeper's play will sensibly improve in a very short time, as he will thereby become accustomed to exercise rapid judgment, and also quickness of sight. One thing which often happens to a goal-keeper is a sudden obscuration of sight after going under water. This can be at once remedied by rubbing the eyelids, and thus preventing the water remaining on the body from dropping over the eye. To all players this hint may be of service. When likely to be tackled by the opposing forwards, the goal-keeper should either pass out to the backs or give away a corner. He must never get flurried, or a goal is certain to be scored against him. When free throws are being taken by the opposing side, a sharp look-out should be kept so as to avoid being hit by the ball. When close in, this trick is often resorted to and a goal scored, as the rule which compels the touching of one other player by the ball before scoring from a free throw is thereby complied with.

### PRACTICE OF A TEAM

If it be found impossible to obtain the assistance of friendly teams for practice games, or a second team from the club be not available, a good system of practice is that adopted by several leading combinations. Only one goal is used, and only one half of the field of play. The goal-keeper, backs, and half-back defend, whilst the three forwards attack. If the ball be thrown beyond half-way, the centre forward is allowed a free throw. The goal-keeper starts the practice by throwing the ball out, the others having taken their positions as in the ordinary game. This is also the procedure after the scoring of a goal. In many cases this is a better plan than having another team from the club, because very often the second-rate players insist upon having one or two of the first team in their ranks, and the practice, as far as the improvement of the combination is concerned, is spoilt. A referee should in all cases be appointed to see that the players conform to the rules.

### HOW TO THROW THE BALL

As may be easily imagined, ability to throw the ball and pass it accurately only comes with practice, and no amount of description will assist a feeble player. A few hints as to the various methods may, however, be useful.

If, when using the breast-stroke, the player desires to pass the ball back, the hand should be placed under it and the arm quickly raised. As soon as the arm is above the surface, it is thrown over the head rapidly, and the ball forced to travel high or low, according to the distance and direction in which it is required to be sent. Either hand can be used, but it is always best to throw with the arm which is farthest away from the nearest opponent. When throwing, a stroke with the legs should be taken, and the disengaged arm forced downwards, to stop the slip given to the body by the throw. If this be done well, it will enable the player to apply more force to the throw or pass.

The throw from the shoulder or side of the head is a very

THE PASS BACK

old plan, and is generally used when a deliberate shot can be taken. The ball is picked up and carried to the shoulder, being held somewhat after the fashion of a weight in athletic competitions. It is rested against the side of the head for accuracy of aim and the better send-off that is obtainable, and is then sent forward with as much force as possible. The legs and disengaged hand are driven down rapidly in the water, and the body shot forward as the aim is taken. A development of this throw is the *ricochet* shot, which, if properly taken, is vastly puzzling to a goal-keeper. The ball is sent in with all possible speed, and so thrown as to hit the water a few yards in front of goal. Unless force can be imparted to the *ricochet* shot, it is practically giving away points to attempt it.

Another breast-stroke pass is that from side to side with either hand when outstretched. The hand is turned with the palm outward and placed under the ball, which is at once lifted out. This is a valuable pass when pressed, especially if it can be done with right or left hand.

The pass, when swimming on the side, is managed by placing the hand under the ball. In this position it can be thrown straight back, and, with practice, to the blind side of the body as well as out to other side. To pass to the blind side, the arm, when it rises with the ball, must be rapidly forced over the body, and the impetus to the ball given from the lower part of the forearm, wrist, and hand. Many players can perform this difficult pass so accurately as to know almost exactly in what part of the field of play the ball will fall.

THE SHOULDER THROW

There is plenty of scope for a back-swimmer at water-polo, especially when long shots are required. The body is thrown back, and the arm outstretched. As the legs are closed, the arm shoots forward, and the ball is driven at a great pace.

As before stated, the 'Trudgeon' stroke offers the best opportunities for a brilliant water-polo player. The overarm

THE BREAST-STROKE PASS

THE OVERARM PASS

pass can be done with either hand, and the ball placed without the player having to turn round for aim. The arms are so

placed that the pass out to right or left can be accomplished
instantly, and the disengaged arm and legs used to maintain
steadiness. With the 'Trudgeon' stroke the ball may be punted
rapidly up or across the bath, the player at the same time being
free from tackling, because in punting the ball is driven forward by either hand, as the player swims, and is not held.
This stroke is again of essential service in dribbling, which is

THE BACK THROW

accomplished by allowing the ball to get between the arms.
Then, as the swimmer progresses, the ball goes with him, it
hitting first one arm and then the other, or the chin, but not
getting out from between the arms.

There are many other little points of the game which come
naturally after a time. The sending out of play or into touch,
if we may use the term, is sometimes of use, although it requires judgment. The rapid hitting of the nearest player with
the ball when awarded a free throw, in such a manner as to

make it rebound to advantage, is also another of the many points which can only be learnt by playing the game.

## THE REFEREE

If there be one thing more than another that causes disputes among clubs, it is the appointment of inefficient referees. A referee should be cool and impartial, of known capability, and thoroughly self-confident. Unless he be the latter he is not of much use, as his decisions will be given with hesitation, and generally objected to.

A referee should first of all satisfy himself that the ball is of the proper size, that the dimensions of the goal-posts are correct, and that they are fixed at least one foot from the end of the bath or any other obstruction. He should then check the depth of the water, and measure the length and width of the field of play, taking care that half distance is marked by some visible object.

After this he should ascertain that the captains have agreed upon all preliminaries, if not, give a decision as the rules allow him to do, and insist upon all players wearing distinctive coloured caps, as well as otherwise conforming to the rules. Particular care should be taken by him that the officials are in their places, and that the goal-scorers are informed that their duties are to signify by means of a flag when the entire ball has passed beyond the goal-posts and under the bar, no matter how passed through, as well as to keep the scores at their respective ends. Before starting the game he should see that the goal-scorers are provided with flags, and be careful to have a proper timekeeper who is thoroughly conversant with the rules. If possible, one side of the field of play should be clear, so as to permit the referee to follow the game from one end of the course to the other.

The absolute control of the game is in the hands of the referee. All cases of misconduct by players should be reported by him to the district association, so that they may be dealt with in accordance with the rules governing meetings, and further, any swimmer who may interfere with or insult the referee during the game, or after, should be reported.

The following hints for referees may be of service :

(*a*) A thorough acquaintance with the rules relating to fouls is absolutely necessary, and in awarding fouls there must be no indecision whatever.

(*b*) When once a decision has been given, do not allow any player or spectator to question your ruling ; for the laws of the A.S.A. definitely state how protests shall be made.

(*c*) See that the resting clause be not abused. The rules only allow standing on the bottom for the purpose of resting, and players must not be allowed to walk about, stand with the arms extended with the idea of shadowing or molesting any player, or jump from the bottom.

(*d*) As to the conduct of matches, the rules governing the water-polo championship should be used as the basis of any decision, when applicable.

(*e*) Goal-keepers must not be allowed to throw the ball past the half-distance mark under any circumstances. If the ball, when thrown by the goal-keeper, travels past half-distance, even if it touch the water before reaching half-distance, the rule is thereby infringed.

(*f*) Note that dribbling or striking the ball is not holding, but that lifting, carrying, pressing under water, or placing the hand under or over the ball when actually touching, is holding.

(*g*) See that no player holds the rail or side during any part of the game.

(*h*) When a goal-keeper or any other player, except in the case of free throws, puts the ball through his own goal, it must be at once signified by the goal-scorer, and declared a goal to the opposing side.

(*i*) Note that a goal cannot be scored from a free throw unless it has touched at least one other player. It does not matter to which side the player belongs.

(*j*) Be careful to award all corner throws to the proper side. It is a corner throw when the ball passes off the goal-keeper behind his own goal-line.

(*k*) When a ball goes out of play the last player it *touches* must be deemed as having sent it out of play.

(*l*) Be particularly stringent with regards to wilful fouls. Only caution the players once, and then enforce the penalty. When advantage is taken of the rule which awards a foul for holding the rail in order to prevent the scoring of a goal, do not allow it, but caution the player, and for a second offence order him out of the bath.

(*m*) Note the rule as to 'leaving the water, or sitting or standing on the steps.'